The Story of the Buddha is part of a series of eight books. These have been published to accompany the series **Animated World Faiths** first shown on Channel 4 in Spring 1998 and in Welsh on S4C over Christmas 1997.

The programmes in the television series were animated using various techniques by some of the most exciting and progressive animation studios across the world – in Hungary, Poland, the Czech Republic, the UK and India.

The scripts have been written by a team of the best children's writers who are adept at combining sound religious and educational content with a lively narrative. The content and language level are carefully aimed at 7–11 year olds.

This series of books accompanies the *Animated World Faiths* series of programmes. The series was commissioned by the Channel Four Television Corporation and S4C (Channel Four Wales).

Book Credits

First published in Great Britain in 1998 by Channel Four Learning Ltd.

Text © 1998 Channel Four Learning Ltd.
Illustrations © 1998 Channel Four Learning Ltd/Longin Studio

Written by **Sally Humble-Jackson**
Design **Holly Mann** and **Tim Shore** of **John Burke Design**
Editor **Christine Alford**
Series Editor **Penelope Vogler**

ISBN 1 862 15245 4

Animation Credits

The Story of the Buddha is based on the animations,
The Life of the Buddha by Longin Studio, Poland; and **The Way of the Buddha**
by TV Studio of Animated Film, Poland
Producers **Ryszard Palonek** and **Andrzej Malaga**
Animation director **Longin Szmyd**

Series Editors **Martin Lamb, Penelope Middelboe, Emma Taylor,
Megan Thomas, Venetia Hawkes** (Right Angle)

Script **Penelope Middelboe** and **Martin Lamb**
Advisors **Dr Vayu Naidu** and **Dr Chris Arthur**

Education Officer **Christine Alford** (Channel Four Learning)

Commissioning Editor **John Richmond** (Channel 4)
Series Executive Producer **Christopher Grace** (S4C)

Animated World Faiths © S4C/Channel 4 Television Corporation MCMXCVII

The Story of
the Buddha

How many years has the Earth been round?
How many times has it turned around?
How many creatures have been born and died
On our dear Earth since the start of time?
The mayfly lives for just one day.
The elephant lives to be old and grey.
Each has a spirit which never dies.
Our spirits are as old as our world.
They turn and turn with the turning of the Earth.
Day after day since the start of time.

Over two thousand years ago, a prince was born to a proud king who ruled over a part of India. The king showed his new-born son to a Wise Man.

'When we die,' said the Wise Man, 'we are reborn. If we are good in one life, we will be rewarded in the next.'

He picked up the baby and looked at him. He looked at his sweet face and his curled fingers. He looked at his tiny feet and his frowning eyes. At last, the Wise Man smiled.

'Your son is very special,' he said. 'He has lived many good lives, so he is ready for a great reward. He will be either a great ruler, or a teacher of Great Truths.'

'He's a prince,' said the king. 'That means he'll be a great ruler.'

But the Wise Man shook his head. 'He must choose. You can't choose for him.'

The king could see that the Wise Man was right. But he did not like it. There had to be a way to make sure that his son chose to rule rather than to teach...

The king thought and thought. How could he stop his son from teaching Great Truths? He decided it would be best if his son never found out about all the suffering and death in the world. That way, he would never ask those questions which can only be answered by Great Truths.

Suppose he kept the boy inside the palace walls, away from bad things? If he gave him everything he wanted, he'd never want to leave.

So little Gotama grew up in a perfect world. Before he woke, the gardeners cleared away the dying flowers. Every night the servants checked that no one in the palace was getting ill, or getting old. Every day the prince ate only the finest food, drank the sweetest drinks, listened to the loveliest music, heard the happiest stories.

Even the prince's horse was sent away when he went lame. 'Just until he's better,' the king explained to Channa, the groom. 'Don't let the prince see him in pain.'

Prince Gotama should have been the happiest person alive. But as he grew to be a man, he became troubled. He wanted something – but what was it?

Then one day he was walking in the gardens when a bird flew up and soared over the palace wall.

Ah! Now the prince knew what he wanted.

'I'd like to go out,' he said to Channa. He smiled. 'Get my horse ready. I'm going for a ride.'

Channa knew the king would be angry – but he was only a servant. He had to do as the prince said.

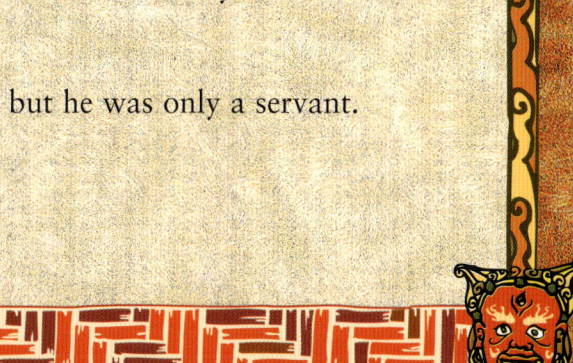

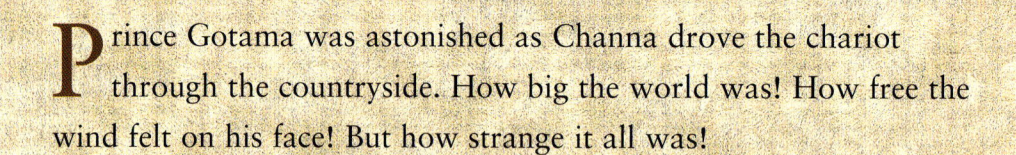

Prince Gotama was astonished as Channa drove the chariot through the countryside. How big the world was! How free the wind felt on his face! But how strange it all was!

Suddenly Channa stopped the chariot. An old man was hobbling across the road. Gotama burst out laughing. 'Why does he move like that? Is he dancing? And who painted his hair white and drew those lines on his face?'

Channa bit his lip. 'He's just old.'

'Old?'

'Everyone gets old. Our skin wrinkles and our hair turns white. We become weak and slow.'

Gotama was shocked. 'Everyone?' he asked. 'But why? Why do we have to get old?' Channa shook his head. He didn't know.

A little way further along, they came across a man moaning with pain. 'He doesn't sing very well,' Gotama sighed.

'He's crying out with pain,' Channa explained. 'He's sick.'

'Sick?'

'His body isn't working properly. It hurts him. Everyone's body can get sick and feel pain.' Gotama was horrified. 'Everyone's?' he asked. 'Even my father's? My wife's? Why? Why must we feel pain?' But Channa didn't know that, either.

The biggest shock of all came when they passed a funeral. The people carrying the body were weeping loudly.

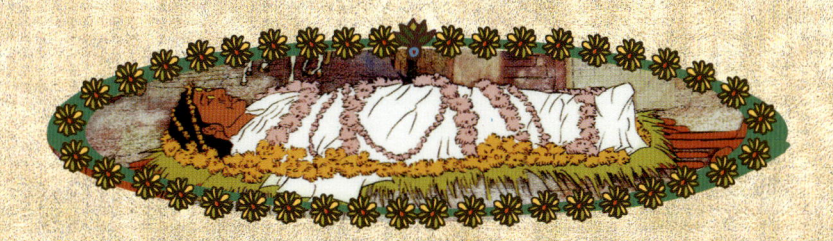

'How can he sleep?' Gotama was very puzzled. 'All that noise...' Channa hung his head. 'He is dead, my Prince, not asleep. His life has gone.'

'Dead?' The prince looked and looked, unable to believe his eyes. 'Gone?'

'Everyone dies in the end. Every living thing.'

'Everyone?' Gotama could feel tears stinging his eyes. 'But why?' he whispered. Then he too hung his head. 'Take me back, Channa,' he begged.

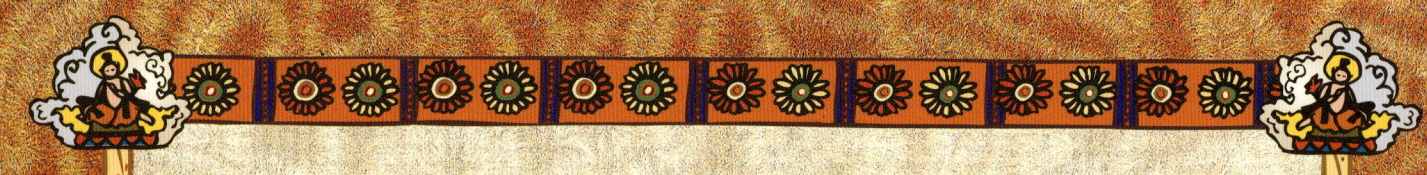

Now that Gotama had started asking questions, he couldn't stop. 'Why didn't you tell me about life outside?' he asked, as his father came hurrying towards him.

'I wanted you to be happy,' the king said.

Gotama closed his eyes. 'I was. But how can I be happy knowing that you'll grow old – or that my wife might get sick?'

'Never mind that. I've wonderful news.' The king rubbed his hands. 'Your wife has just had a baby boy!'

Gotama had looked forward to the birth of his first child for many months. But even the sight of his beautiful new son didn't make him

happy again. All he could think was that this little baby would one day grow old.

That night he went out of the palace gates and sat quietly, wondering why there had to be pain, suffering and death in the world.

To his surprise, a man came along, carrying nothing except a bowl for food.

'What are you doing?' Gotama asked.

'I'm looking for the only thing in life that doesn't die. Truth.'

Gotama leaned forward eagerly. 'Have you found it?'

'Not yet. But I've been getting closer since I gave away everything and left home.'

The prince sighed. 'I can't leave home. I have a kingdom to look after.'

'Isn't Truth more important?' said the man.

Gotama frowned. Was Truth more important than duty? Oh, if only he had some answers...

He went again to look at his wife and child. They slept soundly – young and healthy, happy in their perfect world. Could he really leave them to search for Truth?

But could he search if he stayed?

As Gotama left the palace, he thought his heart would break. He loved his family, but if he didn't go, then his life would be wasted. When he had found the answers he would come home and share them. He could not think of a better gift for his son.

Channa rode with him. When they came to the forest, Gotama gave a poor woodcutter his silk robes and put on the man's simple work clothes. Then he gave his sword and his horse to Channa.

'Tell my father I had to choose for myself,' Gotama said sadly.

Then he set off alone.

He met two Holy Men. For two years they taught him how to think deeply. But Gotama knew that this was not enough, so he set off again on his journey.

He was astonished by the next group of Holy Men he met. One stood on one leg, one hung upside down, one stood in the river, one held up two heavy rocks, and the last sat in a circle of fire. Gotama felt hot and tired and stiff just looking at them!

'Why are you doing that?' he asked.

'Listen,' said the man in the river. 'Our bodies are always making us think about the things they want: food, rest, sleep... If we teach our bodies that the answer is "No", they stop asking. That leaves our minds free to search for Truth.' He shivered. 'I want comfort the most – so I'm teaching my body to do without it. What do you want the most?'

'Well... since I left home I've always been hungry.'

'Then you must do without food.'

After six hungry years, Gotama was near death – and he still hadn't found Truth.

He found himself thinking of his son. The boy would be eight now. Ah! it had felt good to be eight. Except one day it had felt different, not like being a child at all. He remembered a festival… a ploughing contest…everybody cheering… Gotama had felt very quiet in the middle of all the excitement. He remembered the birds soaring above, the smell of the earth, the warmth of the sun. It was as if he'd found an answer to a question he didn't understand.

Suddenly Gotama understood that he'd glimpsed Truth that day. And if a happy child could see Truth, then starving himself was pointless.

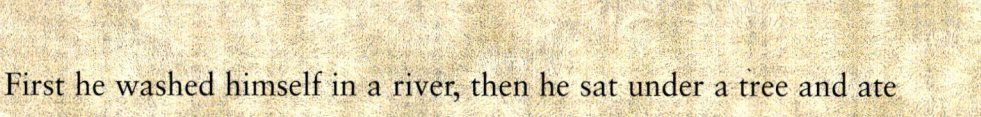

First he washed himself in a river, then he sat under a tree and ate some rice. Well, he understood the questions now. So he'd just stay put until he understood the answers.

Mara, the dark force which tempts us, began to test him then. Mara sent beautiful maidens to fill Gotama's thoughts, and terrible demons to frighten him.

But Gotama wouldn't give in, so Mara planted doubt in Gotama, and made him feel he wasn't good enough to find the answers.

But our dear Earth, the giver of life, came to his aid. She let him remember all his lives since the start of time. He remembered being insects, animals, people... and he saw how each life gave something to the next.

He saw the great wheel of life turning and turning, taking our spirits away and giving them new birth. He saw how greed and hatred and stupidity keep the wheel turning – and how death keeps coming, no matter what.

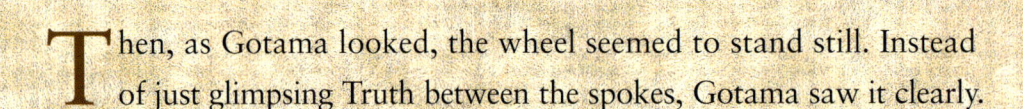

Then, as Gotama looked, the wheel seemed to stand still. Instead of just glimpsing Truth between the spokes, Gotama saw it clearly.

All night long he looked Truth in the eye. He saw that death only has power if you fear it. It will come, but it will pass. There is always new life, just as the Sun always rises and the Earth always turns. He saw that if you stop wanting things, even suffering will pass by. Only old men who want to be young suffer. Only fathers who want to choose for their children get hurt.

By sunrise, Gotama had changed. He'd seen Truth clearly, and that had made him special. Now he was Buddha: an Awoken One.

It was such a special moment that the tree beneath which he sat burst into bloom.

Now he was ready to teach Great Truths. He wanted to teach his family first, but by the time he reached the palace, he already had a crowd of followers with him!

He made sure that he was alone when he met his son.

His son was angry with this stranger who had left on the day he was born. When he saw his father sitting quietly, carrying nothing but an empty food bowl, he lost his temper. He snatched up a handful of sand and dumped it in the bowl.

Buddha said nothing. He just drew in the sand with his finger.

Slowly the boy crept forward to watch.

'This man here,' said Buddha, pointing at his drawing, 'owed money to many people...'

The boy came closer.

'But he didn't want to pay...'

The boy scowled.

'So he left his clothes on the riverbank and set off to swim to the far side. Then people would think he had drowned, and would stop chasing him for their money.

But the river was flowing fast, and he was swept away. He would have drowned if a beautiful golden deer hadn't heard his cries.

The deer leapt into the water and dragged him ashore. It was very dangerous, and the deer had to be very brave. But at last they were both safe.

The man promised he'd never forget the deer who had saved his life. Now he could make a fresh start – though it would be difficult without money.

He had just set off when he met a hunter.

"Are you coming to the Royal Hunt?" asked the hunter. "There's a beautiful golden deer nearby, and the king has offered a reward to whoever kills it."

"Would the king give me the reward if I helped him find the deer?" the man asked eagerly.

So the hunter took the man to the king, who was thrilled to have the chance to hunt the deer himself. The man took the king to the riverside, and sure enough, the deer was still there.

'The king was just about to shoot when the strangest thing happened. The deer opened his mouth and spoke.

"Did this man lead you to me?" the deer asked the king.

The king nodded. He lowered his bow. He could hardly shoot a talking deer, could he?

"He knew where I was," said the deer, "because I have just saved his life. Now he is about to take mine."

The king glared at the man. How shocking! Fancy helping to hunt down the very creature who'd saved your life. "Don't worry," the king said angrily. "I'll punish him for you." And he raised his bow again and pointed his arrow at the man.

"Don't shoot," said the deer gently. "Show him mercy: then he'll learn mercy."

Now the king felt ashamed of himself. This animal was kinder than he was – and wiser. He put away his bow.

"Why do you hunt, your Majesty?" asked the deer. "Try to think of better things than chasing and killing. Try to look around at our dear Earth, which gives life to all things. Try to enjoy this moment of this life. That would be better than killing."

Then the deer wandered off and began to nibble the grass – just like any other deer.

From then on, the astonished king tried always to remember the deer's advice. He stopped hunting and started to enjoy being alive. And the astonished man changed, too. He stopped being greedy and cheating people. And he tried hard to show mercy to others when they did wrong.❜

By the time Buddha had finished the story, his little boy was cuddling up to him.

Buddha smiled down at his son. 'What did you think of that deer?' he asked the boy.

'He was kind,' said the child.

'He was,' agreed Buddha. 'And he did what was right, didn't he?' The boy nodded.

'It is so important to do what is right. Always. Even if it's hard.'

'I know that!'

'But you don't know how hard it was for me to leave you when you were a baby. It was very, very hard indeed. But it was the right thing for me to do.' The child frowned. 'Why was it right?'

'Because I left to find a way for everyone to escape suffering. Not just one deer, or one man, or one king.'

'Oh.'

'So, do you understand that nothing could be more important than that? Not even you?'

The boy thought for a long time. And then he nodded. 'Is that why you are a Buddha, Father?' he asked.

'Yes.'

The boy thought some more. 'What happened to the deer?'

Buddha smiled. 'He's here. I was that deer. In one of my past lives.'

Nearly two thousand years have gone by since all this happened. The wheel of life has turned and turned. But because so many people have learned Great Truths from Buddha, maybe it has slowed a little. And perhaps, if ever we make a world without greed or hatred or stupidity, it will stop. Until then, let's enjoy every moment of our lives on our dear Earth – until the end of time.

24